978-1-62265-938-8 (online) 978-1-62265-939-5(paper)   Alya Omar Almutairi

Scientific Research Methods

978-1-62265-938-8 (online) 978-1-62265-939-5(paper)   Alya Omar Almutairi

© Alya Omar Almutairi, 2015

King Fahad National Library Cataloging-in-Publication Data.

Almutairi, Alya Omar

Scientific research methods./ AIya Omar Almutairi .-

Al Madinah Al Munarnnrarah, 2015

145p; 16, 23cm

ISBN: 978-603-01-9485-0

1- Research - methods   2. Research - Title

978-1-62265-938-8 (online)

978-1-62265-939-5(paper)

978-1-62265-938-8 (online) 978-1-62265-939-5(paper)   Alya Omar Almutairi

The road to success is always under construction

978-1-62265-938-8 (online) 978-1-62265-939-5(paper)   Alya Omar Almutairi

PREFACE

This book is designed specifically for graduate students, academics, and other individuals who need to know about the key concepts of 'research' and 'research design' to perform applied research independently. The approach here is to define the concepts of 'research' and 'scientific research', to differentiate between a research 'method' and 'methodology' and to understand the basics of the 'research process/methodology' and its stages.

Moreover, readers will be able to differentiate and examine the differences between research methods. However, research methods are those techniques used to conduct research on a subject or topic. In contrast, research methodology explains those methods that allow research to proceed. Research methods engage specific experiments, surveys, tests and other devices. Research methodologies include the knowledge of the techniques that are used to perform or to accomplish research as well as to conduct experiments, tests, surveys and other critical studies. Hence, research methods aim to find solutions for research problems, and research methodology seeks to use the correct methods to determine solutions.

Finally, readers will understand the basic format of technical research writing and the essential skills required for writing research project reports.

978-1-62265-938-8 (online) 978-1-62265-939-5(paper)   Alya Omar Almutairi

ACKNOWLEDGMENTS

Alhamdulillah, who made each and every phase or process of this book easy and possible for me to accomplish.

I would have not been able to write this book on scientific research methods without Professors in Faculty of Sciences, Taibah University, who challenged and encouraged me through the writing process. They never accepted my work resulting from less than my best efforts. Thank you.

This book is a collection of gathered and sorted materials that I found from different books and articles. Special thanks to all the authors mentioned in the bibliography page. Furthermore, I would also like to acknowledge and extend my heartfelt gratitude to the following persons who shared their personal experiences with me and aided my writing: My Husband and Dr. Aned. I would also like to thank my colleagues in Statistical section for enabling the publication of this book. Without their encouragement and effort, it would not have been possible to introduce this book in the market. At last, I would like to especially thank to President of Taibah University and Vice President for Higher Studies and Scientific Research (Taibah University) for their encouragement and usual support, which enabled me to complete this book.

Al Mutairi Alya O.

Mathematical Department,
Faculty of Science, Taibah University,
Medina.
Saudi Arabia.
amutairi@taibahu.edu.sa

978-1-62265-938-8 (online) 978-1-62265-939-5(paper)   Alya Omar Almutairi

TABLE OF CONTENTS

No.		Page
	Preface	4
	Acknowledgments	6
	Table of Contents	8
	List of Figures	11
	Abbreviations	12
	Definition of Terms	13
1	Introduction	18
2	Research and Scientific Research	23
2.1	Research	23
2.2	Scientific Research	32
3	Steps of the Research Process	35
3.1	Principle Elements in a Potential Idea/ Research Problems	37
4	Research Designs	39
5	Research Method and Research Methodology	44
5.1	Research Methods	45
5.2	Research Methodology	48

5.3	The Stages of Research	51
5.4	Decide on a Topic	53
5.5	Develop an Overview of the Topic	54
5.6	Determine the Information Requirements	55
5.7	Organize the Information	56
5.8	Analyze and Evaluate the Information	57
5.9	Synthesize the Information	58
5.10	Present the Research	58
6	Formulate a Research Question	60
7	The Basic Principles and Methods of Literature Review	68
7.1	Literature Review	69
7.2	Methods for Performing a Literature Review	77
7.3	Research Objectives should be SMART	80
8	Research Variables, Hypothesis and Conceptual Framework	81
8.1	Research Variables	82
8.2	Research Hypothesis	83
8.3	Conceptual Framework	88
8.4	Research Approaches	90

8.5	Quantitative Research Methods	91
8.6	Qualitative Research Methods	93
9	Ethical and Legal Issues in Scientific Research	97
10	Data Collection Tools	104
10.1	Interviews	106
10.2	Observation	109
10.3	Research Focus Groups	112
10.4	Research Questionnaires	114
11	Fundamental Principles of Data Analysis, Presentation and Interpretation	117
11.1	Data Analysis	117
11.2	Presentation	120
11.3	Interpretation	123
12	Fundamental Principles of Research Dissertation	125
13	Summaries	133
	References	140

LIST OF FIGURES

Page		Figure
36	Steps in the research process	3.1
38	Principle Elements in a Potential Idea/Research Problem	3.2
81	Research Objectives	7.1

ABBREVIATIONS

The following symbols, measurement units, and acronyms are used in this book:

Symbols	Meaning
WMA	World Medical Association
NIH	National Institutes of Health
FDA	Food and Drug Administration
GPA	Grade Point Average
IQ	Intelligence Tests
H_0	Null Hypothesis
H_N	Null Hypothesis
H_1	Alternative Hypotheses
H_A	Alternative Hypotheses

978-1-62265-938-8 (online) 978-1-62265-939-5(paper)   Alya Omar Almutairi

NDAs	Non-Disclosure Agreements
TOC	Table of Contents
VS	Versus

DEFINITION OF TERMS

Research: The term research means to gather information on specific theories or ideas to gain better knowledge related to a particular topic.

Scientific Research: Scientific research uses the scientific method and provides scientific information and theories to aid in explaining the main points and properties of a specific topic.

Research Process/Methodologies: Different research processes are involved in conducting scientific research on a specific topic.

Problem Identification: This is the process in which a research question is designed or a problem is identified.

Literature Review: Once the research problem is identified, the researcher makes a proper review of literature that is related to the research problem. A literature review includes studies conducted in the past that are related to the research topic.

Problem Explanation: The problem is thoroughly explained after a literature review has been performed.

Define Concepts and Terms: All of the terms and concepts used in the research study must be defined clearly to avoid confusion in the minds of readers.

Describe a Population: To clearly specify the group of people in the community who are examined in the study.

Instrumentation Plan: Instrumentation plan refers to the plan that is designed for the study. This plan provides a road map for the entire study.

Collection of Data: In this stage, the researcher highlights the process (either primary or secondary data collection) that is adopted to collect data.

Data Analysis: The method, either quantitative or qualitative, used for analyzing the data is highlighted.

1. INTRODUCTION

Research is the search for new and useful information regarding a particular topic using a logical and systematic approach. Research allows us to identify solutions to social and scientific challenges though a systematic and objective analysis. This analysis involves collecting information from various sources, such as books, journals, human participants, and nature, and analyzing the data to generate relevant conclusions that contribute to the existing knowledge.

Scientific research can be defined as an approach to knowledge discovery based on a set of rules defining acceptable knowledge. It is a systematic approach to do things that have not already been conducted. The philosophy of science is a set of rules that defines acceptable empirical knowledge. Practitioners or scientific researchers address four basic areas: rational inference, critical growth, pragmatic action and intellectual honesty. These areas are discussed in detail in this book.

Research design is an additional concept discussed in this book. Research design is similar to an architectural outline or master plan that illustrates how the research should be conducted. The research method and research methodology, two concepts frequently interchanged due to a misunderstanding of the roles of these concepts in research, are also discussed. Simply put, the relationship between the method and methodology is analogous to the relationship between the derma and dermatology, where derma refers to an outer covering or skin, and dermatology is the discipline that studies skin and skin conditions. Similarly, the methods refer to the techniques or processes used to conduct research, whereas the methodology refers to the discipline.

The stages or steps of a research process can be divided into seven steps, which are discussed in this booklet. An understanding of the role of the literature survey is also discussed. Literature surveys help the researcher properly understand the selected problem, determine whether the proposed problem has previously been solved and identify the methods used to examine the problem.

The research topic is an additional concept that is clarified in this text. The research topic represents the subject area of investigation and encompasses a wider subject area than the research question. A research question is a clear, arguable and focused question that forms the center of the research. Research variables, hypotheses, conceptual framework and quantitative and qualitative research approaches are also discussed. Qualitative research is employed to study why certain data are random, whereas quantitative research studies how random the data are.

Ethics are the norms or rules of conduct that distinguish acceptable and unacceptable behaviors; the ethical and legal issues of scientific research are also discussed. Various data collection methods and the basics of data analysis, interpretation, and presentation are also described. The document is then summarized by describing the fundamental principles of writing a research dissertation.

2. RESEARCH AND SCIENTIFIC RESEARCH

This section introduces the concepts of research and scientific research as a type of research.

2.1 Research

Research is the search for new and useful information about a specific topic using a logical and systematic approach. Research allows us to identify solutions to social and scientific challenges though systematic and objective analysis. This analysis involves collecting information from various sources, such as books, journals, human participants, and nature, and analyzing the data to generate relevant conclusions that contribute to existing knowledge.

Research is not limited to science and technology; research exists in various disciplines, such as sociology and history, and frequently facilitates a change in the communities or nations where the research is performed by enhancing the quality of human life. Research allows new information to be discovered or existing information and theories to be revised. Research requires specific activities, such as experimentation, observation, analysis, comparison and reasoning.

Research has various objectives, including the verification and testing of facts, the discovery of new facts, the analysis of a phenomenon to identify cause and effect relationships and the development of new scientific tools, theories and concepts to understand and solve societal problems.

Research problems are typically challenges experienced by a society or scientific community, and research problems can be practical or theoretical in nature. In addition, the governments of numerous countries use research to enhance or discover various facets of their citizens' lifestyles. In addition industries use research to improve the quality of their products or design new products. Research can be used to optimize business performance in industries, to explain social phenomena and to promote the discovery of new materials or living matter.

Research can be categorized into basic and applied research. Basic research focuses on the principles and reasons for a particular phenomenon, which could be an event or process. Basic research is also known as fundamental or theoretical research. Applied research involves finding a solution to certain problems by utilizing well-known theories and principles. Basic research seeks generalization and focuses on basic processes or natural phenomena that relate to pure science. Basic research attempts to explain why things happen and assembles all the facts to provide insight into a particular problem. Basic research reports are generally written in technical language. The following are examples of questions that form basic research: "Why are materials like that?" and "What are they?"

Basic research results frequently form the basis for applied research, which focuses on examining individual cases without seeking to generalize the conclusions. Applied research focuses on any variable that creates the desired difference and seeks to determine how factors can be altered to correct the problematic facts. Applied research reports are generally written in common language, and the results are immediately applicable.

Both basic and applied research can further be categorized as normal and revolutionary research or qualitative and quantitative research. Normal research is performed within an existing paradigm of rules, procedures and concepts. However, when discoveries are realized that challenge the existing paradigm (revolutionary research), a paradigm shift occurs. In this case, a paradigm refers to a set of perceptions and beliefs, including power relationships and action implications. Paradigms are specific to times, places and context. Foucault (1972) describes paradigms as mindsets of the age, which are revealed though the actions and conversations of individuals.

Qualitative research focuses on quality, whereas quantitative research focuses on the measurement of quantities. Additional types of research include action research, explanatory research and comparative research. Action research focuses on fact finding to improve the quality of action in the social world. Explanatory research focuses on discovering an explanation for phenomena. Comparative research focuses on assessing the similarities and differences among events, methods and techniques.

Primary research involves the study of a subject via first-hand observations and primary information sources, such as statistical or historical data. Secondary research involves the study of a subject through the examination of research performed by other researchers and secondary information sources, such as books and publications. The most common types of research models and paradigms are quantitative and qualitative (Creswell 2003).Quantitative research is also known as traditional, positivist or experimental research. In contrast, qualitative research is also known as constructivist, naturalistic or interpretive research. The research model chosen depends on the worldview or assumptions of each paradigm, the training and experience of the researcher, the nature of the problem and the audience of the study.

Research can also be classified as non-experimental or experimental. In non-experimental research (non-manipulative, correlational or observational research), the naturally occurring relationship between two or more naturally occurring variables is studied, e.g., the relationship between IQ and Grade Point Average (GPA). In experimental research, experimental conditions are applied to random subjects, and the researcher manipulates an independent predictor variable.

2.2 Scientific Research

Scientific research can be defined as an approach to knowledge discovery based on a set of rules that define acceptable knowledge. Scientific research is a systematic approach to do things that have not been conducted. The philosophy of science is guided by a set of rules that defines acceptable empirical knowledge. Scientific practitioners address four basic areas:

a. Rational Inference: This area examines the question "when is something true?"Rational inference addresses the inherent difficulty in supporting claims regarding the existence of a universal truth. Sagan's second rule of science (Sagan 1980) states that whatever does not agree with the facts is wrong and must be changed or rejected completely.

b. Critical Growth: This area addresses the issue "If we have more than one explanation, how can we determine which explanation is better?"Critical growth requires the implementation of standards that can be used to determine whether one explanation is better than another.

c. Pragmatic Action: This area addresses the question "How can we put what we know into practice?" Pragmatic action involves determining how to implement a scientific approach into practice.

d. Intellectual Honesty: This area addresses the issue "Why do we do it the way we do it?" Intellectual honesty considers the ability of the scientist to justify the use of science itself.

Scientific research is not an activity; it is a method to obtain new information that is described by a philosophy. In scientific research, we generalize the results from facts, and the conclusions are grounded in paradigms. Scientific research is based on the consensus of results from several researchers and is a deterministic approach to answering research questions.

3. STEPS OF THE RESEARCH PROCESS

1. Getting started: Thinking of an idea/problem
2. Turning your idea into a research question
3. Reviewing the literature
4. Designing the study and assessing and developing the methods
5. Writing your research proposal

6. Obtaining ethical approval

7. Collecting the data

8. Analyzing and interpreting the data

9. Documenting and disseminating your findings

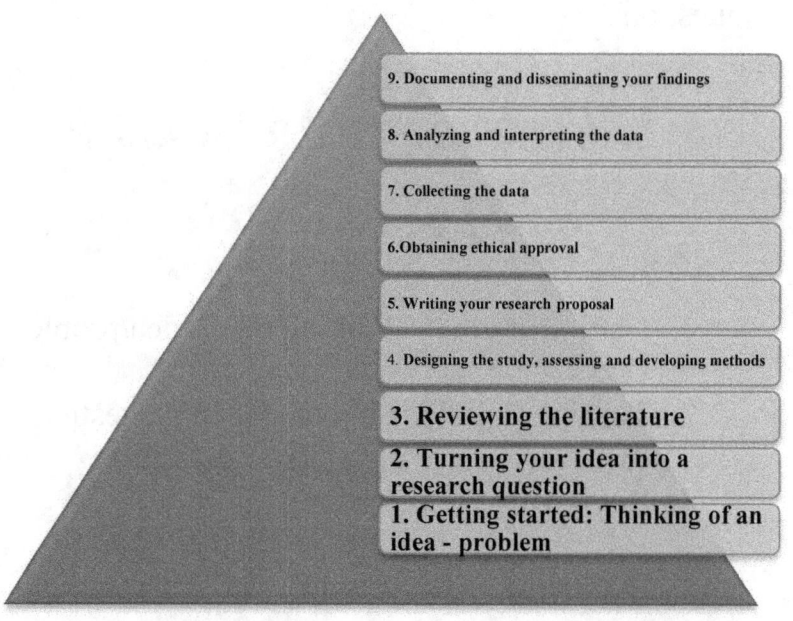

Figure 3. 1 Steps in the research process

3.1 Principle Elements in a Potential Idea/Research Problem

1- Research ideas
2- Personal experiences
3- Literature review
4- Funding opportunity
5- Available expertise
6- Personal interests
7- Public demand

Figure 3.2 Principle Elements in a Potential Idea/Research Problem

4. RESEARCH DESIGNS

A research design is similar to an architectural outline or master plan and describes how the research is conducted. The research design indicates all major components in the research study, e.g., the measurements and sample, and how these components work together to address the research question.

Yin (2003) indicates that "colloquially, a research design is an action plan from getting from here to there where 'here' may be defined as the initial set of questions to be answered and 'there' is some set of (conclusions) answers." In general, two types of research questions are addressed:

- What is happening? This question is categorized as descriptive research.
- Why is it happening? This question is categorized as explanatory research.

Descriptive research can be concrete or abstract. For example, describing the ethical mix of a community is an example of concrete descriptive research because facts and figures can be presented as a result of this research. Determining the amount of poverty in a community is an example of abstract descriptive research. If the descriptive research is performed well, it provokes the why question characteristic of explanatory research.

Explanatory research addresses the why questions to identify the root cause of a phenomenon. For example, it is one thing to describe the crime rate in a country (descriptive research), but it is another to provide a conclusive explanation as to why the crime rate is high or why particular types of crime are increasing or more prevalent.

The concepts of descriptive and explanatory research are important. The research design depends on which model is being used because the model affects the specific information collected. A research design ensures that the evidence obtained sufficiently and objectively provides a convincing answer to the initial research question; therefore, when designing research, it is important to identify the evidence needed to answer the research question. In short, the primary aim of the research design is to limit the ambiguity of the research evidenced. Yin (1989) indicated that the research design addresses a logical problem and not a logistical problem (Yin 1989).

One key issue to note is that the research design is different from the method by which data are collected, i.e., the design logic is independent of the data collection method. Several design types include experimental, case study, longitudinal and cross sectional designs.

5. RESEARCH METHODS AND RESEARCH METHODOLOGY

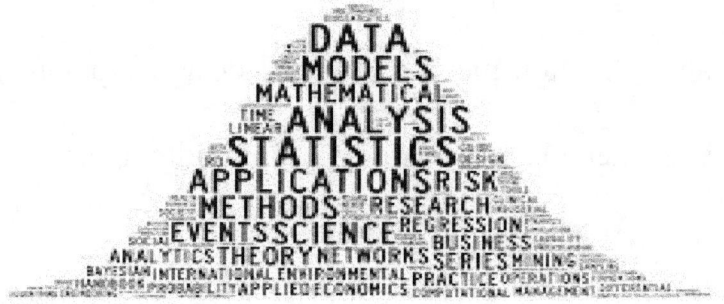

The research method and research methodology are two research concepts that are frequently interchanged due to a misunderstanding of the roles of the two concepts in research. The relationship between a method and the methodology is analogous to the relationship between derma and dermatology, where derma refers to an outer covering or skin, and dermatology is the discipline that studies skin and skin conditions. Similarly, the methods refer to the techniques or processes used to conduct research, whereas methodology is the discipline that utilizes such methods. Next, we discuss methods and methodology.

5.1 Research Methods

Methods are useful to identify the relationship between concepts or parameters in a model. Methods are used to collect samples or data and to identify a solution to a problem. Various methods reveal the significance or extent of the relationships to draw conclusions. Theoretical procedures, numerical schemes and experimental studies are classified as methods that are essentially value neutral; all methods used to execute research are termed research methods.

Some examples of methods used in research include survey questionnaires and in-depth interviews. The method applied is highly dependent on the theory applied, the methodology used and the respective domain applied. Methods and techniques are often interchanged; however, techniques refer to specific aspects of methods. For example, when we consider the method of survey questionnaires, two techniques include close-ended and open-ended questions.

It is also important to note that scientific research methods collect facts, measurements and observations, which are subsequently used to generate an explanation. Reasoning is not exclusively used.

5.2 Research Methodology

Research Methodology

Methodology can be defined as the science of studying how research is performed. Methodology is a systematic way to solve a problem. Research methodology is used to define what constitutes research activity, what methods are applied, and how to measure progress and the success criteria. The research methodology specifies and structures the research results and indicates how to communicate an area of research activity, i.e., the research methodology is an outline of the research work. The methodology is used to describe how researchers will proceed with explanations or predictions regarding the phenomena that are the research focus.

Various types of research methodologies, as described by Walliman (2001), are available, such as historical, comparative, descriptive, correlative, experimental, evaluation-based, action-based, ethnogenic, feminist / identity politics and cultural methods.

Triangulation is defined as a situation that requires the combinations of methods and methodologies to study the same phenomena. One key assumption in combining methods is that any bias associated with one particular method or methodologies is eliminated when combined with other approaches. In addition, methods can be combined for the following reasons: various methods may allow different facets of a phenomenon to emerge, the emergence of contradictions and fresh perspectives, and the first method could aid the second method. When combining methods of data collection and analysis, two approaches can be used: a within methods approach and a between methods approach. In the within methods approach, various data collection strategies are used for the same model. For example, the survey and experiment, which are both quantitative data collection strategies, can be used. In the between methods approach, both qualitative and quantitative data collection procedures are used, such as surveys and interviews.

5.3 The Stages of Research

The research process refers to the procedure of developing a research idea that consists of several steps, including identifying your ideas, assessing and analyzing the ideas and expressing the ideas and/or your results. In an ideal world, these steps occur in a sequential manner; however, it is occasionally necessary to revise and review several steps during research. The research process can be divided into seven steps or stages, which are discussed next.

5.4 Decide on a Topic

The first step in research is to identify the topic and research question. The sources of a research topic include daily problems, technological changes, recent trends and unexplored areas. A topic can refer to a broadly defined subject area, i.e., the effects of obesity. Once a topic has been defined, the research question is used to narrow the topic focus by formulating a series of questions, i.e., "What are the effects of obesity in youth from ages 10 to 15?" We obtain the thesis statement from the research question. The thesis statement indicates the points that will be argued in the question or the anticipated answers. The following is an example of a thesis statement: obesity in youth from ages 10 to 15 causes health difficulties in later years due to limited physical activity/exercise.

5.5 Develop an Overview of the Topic

Developing an overview of the topic is the second stage. In this step, the researcher gathers general background information to refine the topic. An overview also aids in the identification of additional keywords and other resources used to create a general bibliography. Information for the overview is obtained from literature reviews of relevant documentation, including books, publications and other articles.

5.6 Determine the Information Requirements

Once an overview of the information is available, the researcher can identify the information requirements of the research question and determine where to find this information. At this stage, a researcher identifies the resource options and selects the tools that can be used to perform the research.

5.7 Organize the Information

When the appropriate tools have been identified and implemented, relevant data are gathered. It is important to note that before organizing the information, the researcher should verify that sufficient information has been collected. After organizing the information, the next step is to organize the data for analysis.

5.8 Analyze and Evaluate the Information

Once sufficient information or data have been collected, the data need to be analyzed or sorted depending on the research topic or question. This process allows the researcher to identify patterns and draw relevant conclusions.

5.9 Synthesize the Information

The analyzed information can be used to refine the research document.

5.10 Present the Research

The research results are communicated to relevant communities or recipients using an appropriate format or tools, including proper citations.

An alternative process has been defined (Fang 2008) that employs the following steps: identify a problem, review the literature, evaluate the literature, note the ethical issues, note all cultural issues, state the research question or hypothesis, select the research approach, determine how to measure the variables, select a sample, select a data collection method, collect and code the data, analyze and interpret the data, write the report and disseminate the report.

6. FORMULATE A RESEARCH QUESTION

Significant differences exist between a research topic, idea, or problem and a research question. (Research ideas, research topics, and research themes are similar). You may have identified your topic, but you must identify a question within that topic. In addition, you may already have a research question that needs to be converted into a topic.

A research question is a statement that identifies the phenomenon to be studied and should be followed by a question mark.

Well-crafted questions guide systematic research planning. Precisely formulated questions enable the researcher to design a study that has a high probability of answering the questions (Light, Singer, Willett, By Design (1990)).

In research, it is important to clarify the relationship among the research topic, question and title. The research topic represents the area of investigation for the subject and encompasses a broader subject area than the research question. A research question is a clear, arguable and focused question that serves as the cornerstone of the research. The following is an example of a clear research question: How does glacial melting affect penguins in Antarctica? In this case, the topic could be environmental changes due to global warming. The research title is used to inform the readers about the research and is generally used to attract the reader's attention. The following is an example of a title for the research question: "The iceberg is melting."

All research begins with a research question. An ideal research question possesses the following major features: relevant, focused, specific, clear, simple and interesting.

When performing research, it is important that the final research question generated remains within the boundaries of the research topic initially selected or maintains relevancy to that topic. The research question should also be interesting to other individuals in the research field and well grounded in current literature.

In addition, a research question should be specific and focused. It should establish a clear purpose for the research in the selected field. It is important that the research question is capable of being addressed by researchers; for example, if the research requires access to particular individuals or documents, the researcher should have access to the individuals or documents. Resources and time are other key limitations in this area. The researcher should be able to commit the required resources and time to address the research question. Research questions require sufficient scope, and the scope requirements should be balanced with the available resources and time.

A research question that is too complex can lead to an unclear research process. The ambiguity can be attributed in part to unclear thoughts about the research. The research question should be as simple and clear as possible given that ambiguity or contradicting concepts cannot be hidden. In addition, a clear research questions aids in the formulation of a clear hypothesis.

In addition, if the research question is not interesting, the researcher may find it difficult to complete the research, citing boredom and lack of interest. The following two traps should be avoided when selecting a research question: selecting convenient questions and selecting research questions based on currently prevailing situations. In the latter case, the research can become tedious if the situation changes.

Various types of research questions can be asked. It is important to understand the question type to generate appropriate hypotheses and designs. The various types of research questions with their focus areas are summarized below:

- Existence –Does X exist?
- Description and classification –What are the characteristics of X?
- Composition–What components make up X?
- Relationship –Is there a relationship or association between X and Y?

- Descriptive/Cooperative– Is group X different from group Y?

- Causality –Does X prevent, cause, or lead to changes in Y?

- Causality/Comparative – Compared with Z, does X cause more changes in Y?

- Causality/Comparative interaction– Compared with Z, does X cause more changes in Y under certain conditions?

When formulating the research question, the questions should be stated in a question format using detailed and precise terms. In addition, all assumptions should be listed and ambiguities removed before the solution is examined for feasibility. Defining the research question is a critical part of the research.

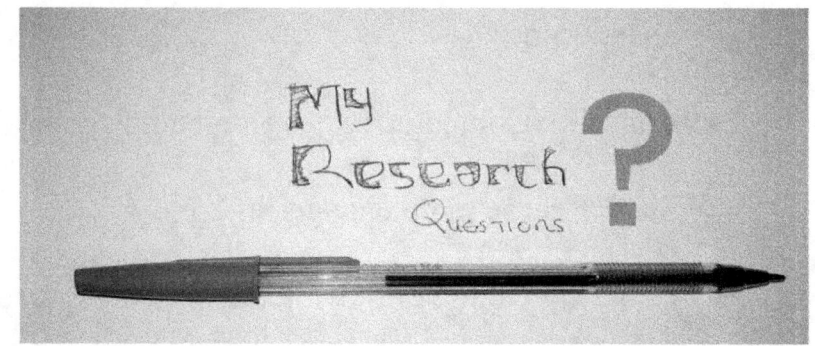

7. THE BASIC PRINCIPLES AND METHODS FOR A LITERATURE REVIEW

A literature review is a systematic survey of scholarly articles, books, and other sources (e.g., reports, dissertations, and conference proceedings) that are relevant to a particular research topic.

A literature review is used to write a review paper, the introduction or background of a research paper, a masters/PhD dissertation, or a proposal for a new area of research.

7.1 Literature Review

➢ Background knowledge on the field of inquiry, i.e., the research question and its components:

- Scholarly facts and figures

- Reference to leading scholars/papers in the field

- State-of-the-art knowledge on the research topic

- Different parameters and perspectives to be studied

- Define key ideas and terms

- Scope for extensions, comparisons, and applications

➢ Knowledge of common or popular methodologies in the field; the relevance, usefulness and appropriateness of methodologies for the study conditions

A literature survey or review refers to the collection of books, research publications and other documents related to the defined problem. Various materials, such as journals, advanced books, and conference proceedings, can be used to obtain data about the subject. A literature survey helps the researcher properly understand the selected problem, decide whether the proposed problem has been solved and determine the methods used to address the problem. A literature survey provides the researcher with the proper theoretical and practical knowledge required to investigate the problem and relates the problem to previous research. The literature review provides a history of the problem and major perspectives of other researchers who have addressed the topic.

The literature review is a critical component of research; it demonstrates the knowledge the writer possesses in the area and justifies the researcher's proposed study. The literature establishes the context for the research and is also used to distinguish important and trivial issues. Upon completion of a literature review, the conclusion must be directly related to the research question. In addition, the conclusion should summarize what is known and unknown. The literature review should also identify areas of controversy in the literature and formulate questions that require further research.

Caulley (1992) indicates that a literature review should compare and contrast the views of various authors on an issue, criticize aspects of the methodology, group authors with similar conclusions, note areas of disagreement, highlight research gaps or exemplary studies and demonstrate the relationship between the current study and previous studies and/or the general literature.

The following key tools and techniques convey the correct message in a literature review:

1. Definitions: These ensure that the reader and researcher begin with the same meanings. When keywords or concepts are used in the literature review, it is important to provide an appropriate definition. In addition, definitions can be used to stipulate what something is or is not.

2. Examples: Examples are used to make a concept more concrete for a reader and enhance the understanding of the definition.

3. Acknowledge critics: Critics who support your views should also be indicated in the literature review to provide a comprehensive view of the research subject or topic.

Writing a literature review is an iterative and recursive process. As more research is conducted, the idea is refined. Drafts are written and revised until the final product is ready for submission.

Three organizing principles can be used to write a literature review: thematic, where the review is organized around a topic or issue; chronological, where the review has different sections for vital time periods; and methodological, where the review focuses on the methods used by the researchers. In addition, the structure of the review generally has three main components: the introduction, body and conclusion.

The introduction identifies and introduces the topic; it explains the criteria for analyzing and comparing data. The introduction also outlines the importance of the topic and summarizes the scope of the literature. The body is a discussion of the reviewed literature based on the organizing principles. For example, in the thematic model, the body is separated into paragraphs, and each paragraph represents a different theme. Finally, the conclusion summarizes the main agreements and disagreements; it identifies where the research fits in the existing literature. When writing a literature review, it is important to use linking words, such as similarly, in addition, and also, to indicate similar concepts. The words however, conversely, or on the other hand should be used to indicate disagreement.

7.2 Methods for Performing a Literature Review

A common method used to perform a literature review involves an initial discussion of broad issues related to the research. Then, the focus is narrowed to issues that overlap with your research. Finally, research that is directly related to your specific investigation is discussed. It is also important to note that the review should primarily focus on issues that are directly related to your research.

To begin the literature review, the researcher needs to understand what information is required to perform the research. Thus, it is important to address the following questions: Does research on this topic already exist? Are there any additional sub-areas of the topic that need to be explored? Is any additional relevant research available? What overlap exists between the sub-topics and other research on the current topic?

When conducting a literature review, it is beneficial to ask some of the following questions for each document that is reviewed: Has the author formulated a problem/issue? Is the problem clearly defined? Is the scope or significance clearly illustrated? Could the problem be more effectively addressed from a different perspective? What is the author's research orientation, e.g., interpretive and theoretical framework? Has the author evaluated the literature relevant to the problem/issue? How is the book/article related to the current research?

Searches using online tools, e.g., Google Scholar, can be useful for identifying information relevant to the literature review. In addition, database/library searches can also provide information either online or in paper form. Journal articles detail current information on current research in the field and are a good source of information. Sources of information can also be identified by reviewing the reference lists in books or articles containing related research.

7.3 Research Objectives should be "SMART"

1- Specific

2- Measurable

3- Achievable

4- Realistic

5- Time

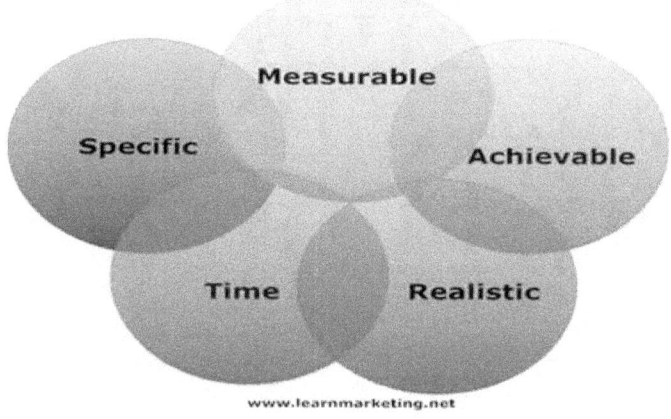

Figure 7.1 Research Objectives

8 Research Variables, Hypothesis and the Conceptual Framework

In this next section, we introduce the concepts of research variables, research hypothesis and the conceptual framework.

8.1 Research Variables

In research, a variable is a subject that can have one or more different values. Age (which can have various values) and gender (which is limited to two values, male or female) are examples of variables. Variables can be either quantitative or qualitative. An example of a quantitative variable is age; age can be assigned various numeric values.

Qualitative variables are also known as categorical or classification variables. For qualitative variables, different values are used to represent the different groups to which a subject belongs. For example, gender is a qualitative value that is represented by one of two values, e.g., male or female.

8.2 Research Hypothesis

Creswell (1994) defines a hypothesis as a formal statement that presents the expected relationship between an independent and dependent variable.

Kerlinger (1956) defines a hypothesis as a conjectural statement explaining the relationship between two or more variables. A hypothesis and a research question are related in the fact that a research question can be considered a hypothesis asked in the form of a question. The hypothesis clearly indicates what will be investigated and identifies the key abstract concepts and research objectives. The hypothesis also indicates the relationship between the literature review and the problem statement, and it is a statement regarding the predicted relationships among events/variables.

A hypothesis can be tested to determine whether it is true. A hypothesis is useful even if proven false. A hypothesis should not be too specific or too general.

Two types of hypotheses are used in research: the null hypothesis, which is typically designated by H_0 or H_N, and the alternative hypothesis, which is typically designated by H_1 or H_A. The null hypothesis represents a theory that is proposed because it is either used as the basis for an argument or it is believed but has not been proven. The alternative hypothesis is the opposite of a null hypothesis, and it is only accepted if the null hypothesis is rejected. For example, if the aim of a clinical trial is to compare the performance of a new drug versus an old drug, the following null hypothesis could be used:

H_0: On average, no difference is observed between the drugs.

The following alternative hypotheses H_1 could be used:

H_1: On average, the two drugs have different effects.

H_1: The new drug is more effective than the old drug.

Once the test has been performed, the result is always presented in terms of the null hypothesis, i.e., H_0 is rejected in favor of H_1, or H_0 is not rejected. The hypothesis depends on whether a qualitative or quantitative research project is being conducted. A hypothesis can be tested in four steps. The first step is to state the hypothesis (either null or alternative). Next, the criteria for the decision are established; data are then collected. Finally, we evaluate the null hypothesis. When testing a hypothesis, it is also important to know whether the hypothesis is one or two sided. A two-sided hypothesis indicates that the control and experimental groups are different, but it does not specify the direction of the difference in advance. In contrast, a one-sided hypothesis indicates a specific direction.

It is important to note that two types of errors can occur when evaluating a hypothesis. The first type of error occurs when the null hypothesis is wrongly rejected (type 1 error); the second type of error occurs when the null hypothesis is not rejected when it is actually false (type 2 error).

8.3 Conceptual Framework

In research, the conceptual framework is the system of concepts, assumptions, expectations and theories that support the research. It has been suggested (Miles and Huberman 1994) that a conceptual framework explains the primary area of study, including the key factors, concepts, variables and presumed relationships, using narrative or graphical formats.

8.4 Research Approaches

The two major research approaches are qualitative and quantitative. Qualitative research can be used to study why certain data are random, whereas quantitative research studies how random the data are. In addition, qualitative approaches can be used to understand the meaning of the numerical data provided by a quantitative approach. The two approaches are discussed in the following sections.

8.5 Quantitative Research Methods

Quantitative research is based on the measurement of quantity/amount. In a quantitative research approach, statistical results are presented using numerical or statistical data. This research approach utilizes surveys, experiments and questionnaires to gather data. The variables in a sample of subjects are measured, and then the relationship among the variables is identified.

Quantitative research methods are used to investigate the what, where and when of decision making. Quantitative research is conclusive, i.e., the results allow concrete conclusions to be drawn. This approach is also iterative and follows a deductive research process.

In this method, the world is considered a single reality that is measurable and separate from the researcher. The purpose of the research is to establish relationships among measured variables, and a hypothesis is formulated at the beginning of the research. In quantitative research, the researcher is an objective observer who does not influence the results, i.e., the researcher and research object are independent. The values are value free and unbiased, and the research language is frequently formal and based on established definitions. Using this method, generalizations lead to predictions, explanations and understanding. In addition, accuracy and reliability are achieved through valid and reliable testing.

8.6 Qualitative Research Methods

The qualitative research approach was initially developed to study social and cultural phenomena and focuses on studying the daily life of various groups of individuals or communities in their natural setting. Qualitative research investigates and explores issues surrounding a current problem. The problem characteristics and dimensions are typically uncertain, i.e., this approach uses soft data to obtain rich data (Domegan and Fleming 2007). This research approach investigates the why and how of decision making. Qualitative research is exploratory and aims to establish the feeling and meaning of a situation.

As indicated earlier, qualitative research is conducted in a subject's natural settings. Using this approach, researchers study concepts in these settings and interpret phenomena in terms of the meaning to individuals. Scholars argue that qualitative data are the best approach to research human learning (Domegan and Fleming 2007). Qualitative approaches are becoming increasingly popular as the analysis methods improve and researchers investigate more efficient and effective techniques for gathering data.

Various qualitative data sources, including observation, fieldwork, interviews and questionnaires, are discussed in Meyers 2009. The text also includes direct impressions and reactions from the researcher. In this case, data are obtained from direct observations, e.g., interviews or written opinions.

In the qualitative approach, the results are presented as descriptive data or narration, and the research purpose presents the social situation from the participants' perspectives. A hypothesis does not necessary initiate this research, and the design emerges as data are collected. An inductive reasoning approach is followed; specific information is generalized to situations or future events, and the researcher actively participates in the research.

Qualitative values are biased and value laden. The research language is frequently informal and presented in a personal voice.

9. ETHICAL AND LEGAL ISSUES IN SCIENTIFIC SERVICES RESEARCH

Ethics can be considered the norms or rules of conduct that distinguish acceptable and unacceptable behaviors. Ethics are important in research because they can be used to promote the aims of the work, including truth, accuracy and knowledge. In addition, ethics promote values, such as accountability and mutual respect, essential for collaboration, a key feature of research (Resnik 2011). Ethics ensure that researchers are accountable to the public, i.e., the mistreatment of subjects. However, ethics also generate public support for research because investors are more likely to invest in a project that has integrity and quality. Finally, ethics promote moral and social values, such as animal welfare and human rights. These benefits of ethics have been discussed in more detail elsewhere (Resnik 2011).

Various government agencies and professional associations have specific codes of conduct; some examples of these agencies include the National Institutes of Health (NIH) (National Institute of Health 2013), the Food and Drug Administration

(FDA) (Food and Drug Administration 2013) and the Nuremburg Code and the Declaration of Helsinki (World Medical Association 2013).

Creswell (2003) states that the researcher has an obligation to respect the rights, needs, values and desires of the informants who are participating in the research. Miles and Huberman (1994) also advise researchers to consider the following issues when performing research:

a) Informed consent: Do all the participants have full knowledge of what is involved?

b) Harm and risk: Can the participants be hurt by the study?

c) Honesty and trust: Has the researcher been truthful in presenting the data, including the risks?

d) Privacy, confidentiality, and anonymity: Will the study require a significant amount of intrusion into group behavior?

e) Intervention and advocacy: If participants display harmful or illegal behavior, what should researchers do?

These ethical principles have been previously discussed (Shamoo 2009); the key factors mentioned include honest reporting, objectivity where it is expected or required, consistent and sincere integrity, the avoidance of negligence, sharing data and tools, respect for all forms of intellectual property, protection of all forms of confidential communications, responsible publication, responsible mentoring of students, respect for colleagues, social responsibility by promoting social good, the avoidance of discrimination, the maintenance of competence in the field, adherence to the relevant laws, and proper care for animals and humans when used as subjects in research.

In healthcare services research, the research subjects are typically animals or humans. With regard to animals, ethical considerations require that unnecessary experiments are not performed. When experiments are necessary, proper respect and care should be provided for the animals, and the experiments should be well designed. With regard to humans, various ethical considerations mentioned above are applicable, including taking special precautions with vulnerable populations and minimizing the risk and harm that could be incurred as a result of the research. From a legal point of view, it is important that the researcher is aware of and subject to the laws in the country of operation as well as relevant government or institutional policies.

In the healthcare field, the key challenges to ethical research include a focus on profits by the investing company and an ignorance of the needs of the participants. In the first case, the investors may want to rapidly bring a product to market without doing sufficient research and development, thereby resulting in the release of healthcare products that actually cause more harm than good. Various governmental agencies, such as the FDA, ensure that appropriate testing is conducted; however, these agencies frequently have insufficient resources to be effective, especially in third world countries.

The second challenge is ignorance of the participants' needs. Medical research volunteers frequently have economic challenges that are temporarily addressed by participating in paid research. These volunteers are also frequently ignorant of their rights; thus, they sign disclaimers or NDAs without fully understanding the documents. In studies where volunteers develop side effects, it is difficult to obtain legal recourse. Moreover, in most cases, the companies involved in the research have sufficient resources to sustain a legal battle or to participate in policy making.

10. DATA COLLECTION TOOLS

Data collection methods are used to gather relevant information for the research. The method used is partially dependent on the type of research conducted. Quantitative approaches for data collection generate results that are easy to summarize, compare and generalize. These techniques include face-to-face interviews, questionnaires with closed-ended questions, experiments and clinical trials. In contrast, qualitative data collection methods provide useful information for understanding the behavior or process; open-ended questionnaires and interactive interviews are often used to collect qualitative data. The most common qualitative methods can generally be divided into the following broad categories: in depth interview, document review and observation methods. However, in this book, we focus on the following four methods: interview, observation, research focus groups and research questionnaires. We discuss each of these methods in the following section.

10.1 Interviews

Interviews are referred to as a "conversation with a purpose" by Kahn and Cannel (1957). Patton (2002)

divides interviews into three general categories: the informal conversational interview, the general interview guide approach and the standardized open-ended interview.

The interview method requires personal contact between the researcher and the participant. This method is ideal for determining a participant's attitudes and beliefs. In the interview method, the interviewer can question the participant to obtain more detailed responses, and the participants do not need to know how to read or write to convey their views.

However, the interview method requires a significant amount of time to ensure effective data collection; the interview should be conducted in a specific environment to maintain a participant's focus during the interview, i.e., a quiet area with comfortable seating and minimal distractions. Another limitation of this method is the need for special recording equipment (audio and/or video) and interview transcribing. The interviewer is critical to this method and must be able to project the fact that the participant's views are helpful and useful; the interviewer also needs exceptional listening, probing and personal interaction skills.

10.2 Observation

Observation is a data collection method that involves watching events or behaviors in their natural settings. Observations can either occur overtly, where the participants know they are under observation, or covertly, where the observer is hidden, and the participants do not know they are being observed. Participants are more likely to behave more naturally during covert observation; however, this method occasionally presents ethical challenges. Observation can also be direct, where interactions are monitored as they occur, or indirect, where the results of processes or interactions are monitored. An example of a direct observation is watching students in a school cafeteria to determine if they respond to a new menu in a positive manner. An example of an indirect observation is measuring the plate waste left by the same students to determine whether they have a positive or negative response to the new menu. Observation is useful when the researcher needs to gather data on individual behavior or group interactions and to understand an ongoing process. Observation can also be utilized when it is not feasible to collect individual data.

The observation method is an ideal method to identify behavior patterns, and it is especially useful when the research output requires or includes observable products. Observation allows the researcher to witness event indicators. Observation can provide more reliable data than interviews because the researcher can witness what happened instead of relying on participants to convey what happened or what they think happened.

However, the limitations of this method include the time required to observe and record the observations and the fact that the researcher cannot question the participants during observation. Because this method is susceptible to observer or participant bias, follow-up interviews are occasionally required to verify observations and clarify conclusions.

10.3 Research Focus Groups

Research focus groups involve interviewing a group of individuals at the same time. The advantages of this method are that group dynamics can generate more ideas than individual interviews, and the participants are not required to read or write because all communication is verbal. Focus groups can be used to gather more details about issues raised through other methods, e.g., surveys. Research focus groups are an ideal method to evaluate attitudes and beliefs from a large group of participants at once.

However, a disadvantage of this group-based approach is that the facilitator must guide the discussion in the appropriate direction and ensure participation from all participants. In addition, this method requires set-up time, and it may require special equipment to record and transcribe the discussion. Research focus groups also require the researcher to identify and schedule relevant participants for the focus group, which takes additional time and effort.

10.4 Research Questionnaires

Questionnaires require the participants to complete a form without researcher assistance; thus, the questionnaires can be distributed and collected at a later date.

This approach is best for obtaining written responses on a subject. The questionnaire can include both close-ended questions, which require the participants to select one of the available options, and open-ended questions, which allow the participants to freely express their views. Questionnaires do not necessarily require personal contact given that the forms can be submitted in written form or online. In addition, minimal researchers are required for this method because one researcher can distribute and collect the questionnaires.

The limitations of this approach are that the responses are limited to the questions in the questionnaire and that participants must be able to read and write. With regard to open-ended questions, participants must be able to express themselves clearly to meaningfully impact the research. The questionnaire format should also be simple with no ambiguity; it should not contain concepts or words that confuse the participants. If questionnaires are not worded properly, questions can be misunderstood; thus, time should be allotted to fine tune the questionnaire. Finally, questionnaires rely on the perception and beliefs of the participants; thus, a gap between reality and the participant responses may exist.

11. FUNDAMENTAL PRINCIPLES OF DATA ANALYSIS, PRESENTATION AND INTERPRETATION

This section presents the basics of data analysis, interpretation, and presentation.

11.1 Data Analysis

Statistical analysis of quantitative data are used to measure the degree of change that has occurred or allows statements to be made regarding data consistency. Qualitative data can be grouped into various similar categories to identify meaning. The data analysis phase converts the collected data into evidence that supports the research. Three steps are typically involved in data analysis: preparing the data for analysis, describing the data and interpreting the data. This section describes data preparation and analysis, whereas data interpretation is discussed in the next section. When preparing and analyzing data, the following evaluation criteria can be used:

1. Relevance: Is the data to be prepared still relevant to the research and aligned with the research question?
2. Effectiveness: Did the research methods employed obtain all of the required data?
3. Efficiency: Was the maximum amount of data obtained from the methods?
4. Results/Impact: What was the impact of the research on the research question?

11.2 Presentation

Successful data presentation is determined by the relevance, quality and integrity of the data content. Various methods of data presentation are available, including report writing and power point presentations. Report writing is discussed further in section 15; we focus on presentations in this section. For power point presentations, a few key design principles should be followed and are briefly discussed below.

Good visualization requires good data and detailed analysis. The researchers should be familiar with the data they are presenting. The content to be presented should be carefully selected depending on the message to be conveyed and the audience.

Good visualization should be used to provide a direct answer to specific questions, and the researcher should clearly indicate what questions are being asked. In addition, good visualization enhances data; it does not obscure data. Appropriate visualization should be chosen based on the audience, metrics and chart type.

Other aesthetic considerations include the use of modifying lines, shading or borders as well as fonts and colors that are minimally distracting. In addition, a palette of grays and muted hues should be used to ensure that a black and white copy conveys the relevant information. Contrast can be provided by using minimal high chroma colors. The font style, weight and spacing should be chosen to enhance clarity.

Several mistakes are often made by researchers when presenting data (Tufte 1983). Presentations should begin with a clear message. If the message does not require a graph, then a graph or table should not be inserted. However, if a graph is required, the correct format should be used to effectively communicate your message.

11.3 Interpretation

A key issue in data interpretation is relating the results of the research to the initial research question. Interpretation requires a clear definition of two terms: association and causation. If one event is more likely to occur because another event has occurred, then the two events have an association. However, the first event does not necessarily cause the other event. In contrast, a causal relationship exists when one event is necessary for the second event to occur. The first event is the cause, and the second event is the effect. For example, for a driver to have a car accident (effect), he must first be driving a car (cause).

12. FUNDAMENTAL PRINCIPLES OF A RESEARCH DISSERTATION

When reading a research paper, the reader is generally seeking to answer the following questions:

1. What is the work trying to accomplish and why?
2. What specific contribution is made?
3. Are the contributions genuine?

Some general principles of dissertation writing are noted that allow the reader to answer these question. First, to save time, reading and writing should be performed in tandem, not separately. It is important to fully note any references during this process.

When writing the report, the researcher should manage the reader's expectations by clearly explaining what is described in each section of the report, ideally at the beginning of the section. To allow the reader to easily evaluate the research work, the report should focus on the analysis rather than the description. When the results are presented, the report should interpret and explain what the results mean to the research.

Only honest information that is supported by factual evidence should be reported. The information source should be appropriately acknowledged and referenced. In addition, the research should clearly distinguish between facts and opinions.

The text should be clearly written without using more words than necessary. The research goals and objectives should be indicated. Images and graphs should be used appropriately with the appropriate labels or headings. Punctuation, hyphenation and spelling checks should be performed.

Keywords and concepts that can easily be misunderstood should be defined prior to the use of the keyword or concept. Finally, only information that is relevant to the research should be included, and sufficient references to support your research should be used.

When writing the research, these steps can be followed:

1. Produce a framework that acts as a structural guide and a reference point for the writer and reader, respectively. The framework should include the title, chapter titles, and section/subsection headings.
2. Draft a title that is comprehensive and clear; it should indicate the focus of the research without being too long.

3. Draft a table of contents that indicates all major chapters to avoid repetition or ambiguity. The TOC should be substantive, accurate and relevant.

4. Write the chapter drafts. The chapters can be divided into various subsections with headings to provide information about key chapter information or arguments. The content of each chapter should guide the reader to understand the message that is being conveyed.

The major components of a research report or dissertation are discussed. The introduction establishes the research boundaries and clearly identifies the research focus. The introduction should provide the reader with a high-level summary or synopsis of the work that has been performed. The research/thesis question and the motivation of the work are presented. In addition, the objectives of the research, the contributions made by the author, an overview of the research and a description of the remainder of the paper should be included in the introduction.

The next section is the literature review, which provides relevant information about the research topic. Additional information regarding the literature review is presented in chapter 8. In this section, it is important to clearly indicate the gaps in the literature that the research is addressing.

The literature review is followed by the chapters that discuss various theoretical aspects of the research. After the theoretical chapters, a chapter on the implementation or methodology that provides the context and stages of data collection as well as the rationale for data collection is presented. This chapter also highlights any implementation challenges and how these challenges were managed.

The research results are then presented together with an analysis or interpretation of the results in relation to the initial research focus. Finally, the conclusion section includes recommendations or future work to be performed.

The appendices and bibliography are located at the end of the document. The bibliography and references should be formatted using an appropriate style, and the referencing method should be consistent throughout the document. In addition, all claims in the document should be supported with references.

Dissertation writing is a time-consuming task, and several drafts of the report should be written before the final version is submitted.

13 SUMMARY

This book provides an introduction into research and various key concepts of research. Research is the search for new and useful information regarding a particular topic, and this new information can be used to provide solutions to social and scientific challenges. In this book, the concepts of research and scientific research are presented. We also explain research categorizations, such as applied and basic research, normal and qualitative research and qualitative and quantitative research. Scientific research is a mechanism for acquiring information based on the philosophy of science, which is addressed by four basic areas: rational inference, critical growth, pragmatic action and intellectual honesty.

The research design provides a master plan for the research and includes the major components to be included in the research study. The research design depends on whether descriptive or exploratory research is performed.

The difference between the method and methodology as well as the major stages of a research process are also discussed in this booklet. It is important to note that these stages can be revisited as more relevant information becomes available during the research process. Some key steps include developing the topic; providing an overview; determining the information requirements; organizing, analyzing and evaluating the information; synthesizing the information and presenting the research results.

Following the presentation of the research process, a discussion on the formulation of a research question, the goal of the research question and the key features of a good research question were presented. Once the research question has been identified, an overview of the research is obtained by performing a literature review. The objectives and methods of a literature review were discussed. Three organizing principles can be used when writing a literature review: thematic, chronological and methodological; these principles and the major components of a literature review were discussed.

The research hypotheses, variables and the conceptual framework were discussed. We discussed the two main research approaches: qualitative research, which studies why certain data are random, and quantitative research, which studies how random the data are. The various characteristics of the two methods were discussed, and a discussion on the ethical and legal issues in scientific research followed.

Ethics are the norms or rules of conduct that distinguish acceptable and unacceptable behaviors. In scientific research, ethics promote the values essential for collaborations between researchers and ensure that research is used for the good of the community. Various agencies, such as the National Institutes of Health (NIH) and the Food and Drug Administration (FDA), have codes of conduct to ensure ethical behavior during research; some areas addressed in these codes include respect for all forms of intellectual property, objectivity where it is expected or required and proper care of animal or human subjects in research.

Four data collection tools, i.e., interviews, observation, research focus groups and research questionnaires, were discussed in conjunction with the advantages and disadvantages of each tool. Following data collection, we discussed the steps of data analysis, presentation and interpretation. The book also provided guidelines for writing a research dissertation by examining the questions the dissertation should answer and the general format of the dissertation.

This book was designed to provide individuals seeking to perform research with an introduction to the major research concepts and key issues that should be addressed during research. Further information can be found in the various references cited in the book.

REFERENCES

Creswell, J. W. (1994). *Research design.* Thousand Oaks, CA: Sage publications.

Creswell, J. W. (2003) *Research design: qualitative, quantitative, and mixed methods approaches* Thousand Oaks, CA: Sage Publications

Domegan, C. and Fleming, D. (2007) *Marketing Research in Ireland- Theory and Practice.* Gill and MacMillan Ltd., Dublin.

Durrance, J. C. and Fisher, K. E. (2005) *How Libraries and Librarians Help: A Guide to Identifying User-Centered Outcome.* Chicago: American Library Association

Fang, L., Manuel, J. , Bledsoe, S. E. and Bellamy, J (2008). *Finding existing knowledge.* In

Grinnell, R. M and Unrau, Y. A (Eds), social work research and evaluation: Foundations of evidence-based practice (p 466) Oxford : Oxford University Press

Food and Drug Administration (FDA) (2013) Retrieved from http://www.fda.gov/

Foucault, M. (1972). The archaeology of knowledge. (Tavistock Publications, Ltd., Trans.). London: Routledge (Original work Published 1969).

Foucault, M. (1972-1977). Power/knowledge: Selected interviews and other writings. (C. Gordon, Ed.). New York: Pantheon.

Kerlinger, F. N. (1956). *The attitude structure of the individual: A Q-study of the educational attitudes of professors and laymen.* Genetic Psychology Monographs, Vol 53, 283-329.

Light, Singer, Willett, By Design (1990). http://www.nnyman.com/personal/2005/11/18/the-user-experience-equation/

Miles, M. B., & Huberman, A. M. (1994). *Qualitative data analysis: An expanded sourcebook.* Sage.

National Institutes of Health – Official site (2013). Retrieved from http://nih.gov/

Patton, M. Q. (2002). *Qualitative research and evaluation methods (3rd ed.).* Thousand Oaks, CA: Sage.

Resnik, D. B. (2011) What is Ethics in Research & Why is it Important, Retrieved from http://www.niehs.nih.gov/research/resources/bioethics/whatis/index.cfm

Shamoo A and Resnik D. (2009). *Responsible Conduct of Research, 2nd ed.* (New York: Oxford University Press).

Tufte, E. R., (1983). The Visual Display of Quantitative Information, Graphics Press

Walliman, N. S. R. (2001) Your Research Project: A Step-by-Step Guide for the First-Time Researcher by London: Sage Publications Ltd

World Medical Association- Official site (2013) Retrieved fromhttp://www.wma.net/en/10home/index.html

978-1-62265-938-8 (online) 978-1-62265-939-5(paper)   Alya Omar Almutairi

The book has been Certified as:

1. Clearance Letter from Ministry of Culture and Information in Saudi Arabia and legality to be distributed in Saudi Arabia.

2. Letter certified that the book was edited for English language, grammar, punctuation, spelling, and overall style by one or more of the highly qualified native English speaking editors at American Journal Experts.

3. Turnitin Originality Report, Similarity Report. as the similarity was 2%.

Date & Completed by: 22 Dec. 2015

Author's Profile:

Dr. Alya Al Mutairi received her PhD from the Science University of Malaysia, 2015. In the same year she joined Taibah University as a Professor of Mathematics, where she is now a member of the Applied Statistics Group. The author has several research papers. Al Mutairi is distinguished by School of Mathematics in USM in Publications Research papers. She joined by a several Scientific Fellowships like: RSS, ASA, SSSME and ISOSS. Prior to her academic career, Al Mutairi was ranked first in north-western Region in Intermediate, Secondary and College Subsequently by getting the Highest Grade in the Intermediate School, Secondary and College in North-Western Region in Saudi Arabia, as a high school teacher in the 2001s, she coached students for various mathematical sessions. Al Mutairi is elected a member in the Scientific Group of many Conferences and Scientific Committees. Al Mutairi is published many Scientific research papers in prestigious journals.

www.ingramcontent.com/pod-product-compliance
Lightning Source LLC
Chambersburg PA
CBHW070624300426
44113CB00010B/1644